Developing A Godly Character

A 30 Day Devotional and Journal for Teenagers

ANJLI SHARMA

Cover design: 100Covers.com

ISBN: 978-0-578-81171-0

Dedication

I would like to dedicate this book to God because He has led me to write this devotional to young adults who may or may not know what purity looks like. I thank God for how He has changed my heart, and I know He desires to bring change to the next generation as well.

Matthew 5:8 (AMP) *"Blessed [anticipating God's presence, spiritually mature] are the pure in heart [those with integrity, moral courage, and godly character], for they will see God."*

Introduction

Dear Amazing Teenager,

I thank you for choosing to read this book about what good character looks like. There are a lot of impure motives, intentions, thoughts, and feelings in which people live or get stuck. In this book, you will realize how character on the inside is what counts. Being a teenager isn't easy, as you struggle between being a kid with no responsibilities and becoming an adult with many responsibilities.

I can relate to those teenage struggles, because I went through my teens doing my own thing, not listening to people's advice, being prideful and disobedient to my parents. What God wants you to know is that you don't have to grow this way alone; you can depend on God who can help you through the process to become all that He has created you to become and to pursue a pure purpose! I believe God truly wants to change your heart in the best way—He knows it is possible. I wrote this book because I know God changed my heart to become more and more like Christ.

Christlike Character = Heart Work

I love sharing with young people that are hungry to fill something they know is missing in their lives. I have been chosen for such a time as this to share God's truth so that the truth can set you free. It's up to YOU to accept or reject His truth. The Bible is filled with prophecies (foretelling future events), encouragement, instructions, wisdom, knowledge, parables (stories taken from the culture that teach God's love or principles) and so much more.

It's so difficult as a teen to not be influenced by the opinions of others but let me encourage you to let the Word of God change you instead. We can ask God to change us, but it starts on the inside i.e. the heart. Will you have an open heart to learn what He is speaking to you when it comes to developing good character? The choice is yours!

1 Timothy 4:12 (ESV) *Let no one despise you for your youth, but set the believers an example in speech, in conduct, in love, in faith, in purity.*

~Anjli

Let the words of my mouth and the meditation of my heart be acceptable in thy sight, O Lord, my strength and my Redeemer.

~Psalm 19:14

Day 1

Who Are You to HIM?

Devotional

Have you ever been bullied by someone that said hurtful words and put a label on you saying that's who you are? Those words and labels get stuck in your mind and heart, and you begin to believe the lie that this is who you are.

It can also be the same spiritually when it comes to our enemy. We are also in a spiritual war—a battle for our souls. The devil is our enemy, and he speaks lies and says that's who we are. He uses labels such as: A nobody, unworthy, ugly, too skinny, too fat, too dumb, cursed, etc.

After I accepted Jesus, I was baptized in water. I became a new creature in Christ. It brought me new freedom, joy, peace, and love. A new creature whose identity equals royalty and blessing. My identity is now *in* Jesus. What matters is *who He says I am*. And He calls me *His* daughter. Will you believe the labels from the world? The devil? Yourself? Or will you listen to Him?

Prayer

Father God, I come to You with my heart, seeking a change in my identity. I was lost in a world of labels telling me who I am. Heal my heart from all the ways people labeled me. I want to become more and more like Jesus. Speak to me and tell me who You say I am in Jesus name I ask! Amen!

Application

If you never accepted Jesus in your life and want lasting change from God, it's not too late. You can accept Him in your heart today. Get baptized. Be done with the old life and enter a new life and new identity in Jesus Christ.

Scripture

2 Corinthians 5:17 (AMP) *Therefore, if anyone is in Christ [that is, grafted in, joined to Him by faith in Him as Savior], he is a new creature [reborn and renewed by the Holy Spirit]; the old things [the previous moral and spiritual*

condition] have passed away. Behold, new things have come [because spiritual awakening brings a new life].

Ask God, "who do You say I am?" Journal His response.

_____
_____
_____
_____
_____
_____
_____
_____
_____
_____
_____
_____
_____
_____
_____
_____
_____
_____

Day 2

It's the Inside That Counts

Devotional

What you wear on the outside can also affect how you feel on the inside. Likewise, when you work out and eat healthy food, you are taking care of yourself physically. Not only do we need to care for ourselves physically but also spiritually. Spiritually we have a heart with pure or impure intentions and motives. Pure intentions can lead people right, while impure intentions can lead people wrong.

Prayer

Father God, thank You for creating my heart. Lead my heart to become pure. Check my heart for any impure motives and intentions that displease You. Soften my heart to become more and more like Your heart, God. In Jesus name I ask and pray! Amen!

Application

Daily ask the Lord Jesus to check your heart about things from which you need to repent.

Scripture

Psalms 139:23-24 (AMP) *Search me [thoroughly], O God, and know my heart; Test me and know my anxious thoughts; And see if there is any wicked or hurtful way in me, And lead me in the everlasting way.*

Journal your prayer to God. Seek His guidance in recognizing impure motives.

Request His help in purifying those motives as He softens your heart.

Day 3

Let's Talk About It

Devotional

What we say, how we say it, and who we are saying our words to is a big deal to God. When we have conversations about drugs, sex, alcohol, what's happening in the news, and/or hateful speech to or about people that may have hurt us, we put our mouths in danger of speaking death. On the flip side even the business world today recognizes the power of positive affirmations—claiming for ourselves positive statements as if they are already true about us. It is so much more effective when we are instead claiming the truths of who God says we are—His beloved, His daughters and sons, fearfully and wonderfully made, the apple of His eye, His Holy possession.

Prayer

Father God, I pray that You would give me a new tongue of life and truth. I repent for speaking death to or about anybody that has brought more harm to them and myself. I ask You to search my heart and reveal things I have said that were hurtful instead of helpful. I turn away and I ask You to forgive me. In Jesus name I ask and pray! Amen!

Application

Write and give an encouraging word to someone that is living in a negative mindset or situation. Thank, love, and encourage them today.

Scripture

Proverbs 18:21 (AMP) *Death and life are in the power of the tongue, and those who love it and indulge it will eat its fruit and bear the consequences of their words.*

Do you sometimes speak without taking time to think about the effect your words have on yourself and others? Memorize today's verse.

Journal some steps you could take to help you pause before speaking. List more of the things God says are true of you.

_____

_____

_____

_____

_____

_____

_____

_____

_____

_____

_____

_____

_____

_____

_____

Day 4

What on Earth Are We Listening To?

Devotional

Songs are soothing to the ears and can either give us a positive or negative vibe. The words that come from the songs can either make or break us. What we listen to on the radio, CDs, Spotify, or at a concert can move our bodies, hearts, and minds. We could listen to curse words in a song and start to pick up on the habit of cursing, or we can listen to a song that can change our life forever. Which one would you rather listen to?

Prayer

Father God, I thank You for creating these ears to hear the truth about the songs we listen to everyday. Wipe away any unclean songs from my mind that don't help and heal my soul. Guard my ears from hearing any music that doesn't help me. Help me to listen to the songs that bring my heart, mind, and body healing and encouragement. In Jesus name I ask and pray! Amen!

Application

Start to listen to Christian music on the radio, CDs, and/or a music station like Spotify that plays positive and encouraging songs.

Scripture

Colossians 3:16b (AMP) ...*singing psalms and hymns and spiritual songs with thankfulness in your hearts to God.*

Journal the lyrics of a song that has uplifted and strengthened you.

Day 5

Turn Off the Bad News

Devotional

We all have a favorite movie and/or TV show we love to watch. We may love the excitement of violence, sexual scenes, scary, or dramatic movies. We watch the news that broadcasts all the bad that is happening each day because we are curious to know. All that negativity changes our hearts, minds, and souls. What we see on TV can either depress us or cheer us up. We can pray for the bad news to change. We can be careful what we see in movies or on TV. We have a choice about what we see. Ask yourself, *Is this TV show or movie I am watching helping or hurting my heart?*

Prayer

Father God, I thank You that You watch over us in everything we do, see, and say. I am aware of the shows and movies I watch that can either help or hinder me. I pray that You would change my heart in what I see. Purify my heart so my eyes can see TV and movies differently. In Jesus name I ask and pray! Amen!

Application

There are many great movies and TV shows on PureFlix to watch. Encourage your heart by checking it out.

Scripture

Psalms 112:7 (AMP) *He will not fear bad news; His heart is steadfast, trusting [confidently relying on and believing] in the Lord.*

Are there movies or TV shows you watch that pull your attention away from God?

Jot down titles that you plan to avoid, or ones you need to pray about and evaluate if they are worthwhile to continue watching.

Day 6

What's on Your Mind?

Devotional

Have you ever had a negative thought cross your mind and wondered, *Wow, where did that come from?* We all have good and bad thoughts come to our minds. When we have bad thoughts, we must learn how release them instead of dwelling on them. We can either accept or reject those thoughts.

What we think about either cripples us or cheers us. Our mind is in a war between thinking positive and negative thoughts. We can fight off the negative thoughts by recognizing them and replacing them by reading and applying scriptures from the Bible.

Prayer

Father God, thank You for giving me a sound mind to hear from You. I open up my mind to hear Your thoughts that are pure, true, right, honoring, and lovely. I pray that every negative thought that comes would be eliminated and would come under the subjection of Christ. Renew, cleanse, and purify my mind daily so I can live the life of peace, joy, and love You're calling me to live. In Jesus name I ask and pray! Amen!

Application

As soon as you get a negative thought, write it down on a piece of paper, take that word captive by reading 2 Corinthians 10:3-6 and pray for the Lord to replace it with His positive thoughts.

Scripture

2 Corinthians 10:3-6 (AMP) *For though we walk in the flesh [as mortal men], we are not carrying on our [spiritual] warfare according to the flesh and using the weapons of man. The weapons of our warfare are not physical [weapons of flesh and blood]. Our weapons are divinely powerful for the destruction of fortresses. We are destroying sophisticated arguments and every exalted and proud thing that sets itself up against the [true] knowledge of God, and <u>we are taking every thought and purpose captive to the obedience of</u>*

Christ, being ready to punish every act of disobedience, when your own obedience [as a church] is complete.

Memorize 2 Corinthians 10:5b, underlined above. Write it out, then write your prayer to God asking His help in replacing your negative thoughts with His positive thoughts.

_____

_____

_____

_____

_____

_____

_____

_____

_____

_____

_____

_____

_____

_____

Day 7

Get That Pure Ship On

Devotional

Have you ever gotten into a dead-end relationship and thought, *What did I get myself into?* Have you thought about where your heart has been in the relationship? Have you asked God, *Is this relationship for me?* The question is, do you love or lust this person? We long for love, so we get ourselves into relationships to fill up the void. Don't get me wrong here, God wants us to be with the person He has for us. Waiting on God for the right person He has for us is a blessing. When we aren't fully developed in our maturity—growing, overcoming struggles, learning from our experiences—we rush the process of getting into a relationship that we haven't prepared ourselves for. Prepare yourself for that person God has for you to be with in a healthy relationship.

Prayer

Father God, thank You for loving me so much You want me to be in a relationship that You have for my life. I trust in You God to provide the right person for me in Your time. I pray that You prepare me for the right man or woman that will come into my life. Have it Your way God because Your ways are the best ways to pursue. In Jesus name I ask and pray! Amen!

Application

Get a journal and write down everything the Lord wants you to know about yourself. Ask Him to speak to you and write it down. Wait on the Lord. Seek God by praying, reading the Bible, and worshipping every day.

Scripture

Psalms 27:14 (AMP) *Wait for and confidently expect the Lord; Be strong and let your heart take courage; Yes, wait for and confidently expect the Lord.*

Jot down your thoughts about waiting on God's timing for a relationship.

Include your thoughts on preparing yourself first. Journal a prayer to God.

_____

_____

_____

_____

_____

_____

_____

_____

_____

_____

_____

_____

_____

_____

_____

_____

_____

Day 8

Attitude Changes Everything

Devotional

When I was a teenager, my parents told me to clean "this", take out the trash, and wash the dishes. I had an attitude of laziness and didn't do it. I behaved in a rebellious way toward them. Has there been a time when your parents told you to do something and you rolled your eyes at them like they were crazy? When people tell us to do something, we can react with a positive or negative attitude. It's up to us to choose how we will react to hard and soft situations. How do you respond when you are inconvenienced? How will you react when stormy situations come your way? If you respond poorly in small things, you likely will respond poorly in big things. Allow the Holy Spirit to help you react positively.

Prayer

Father God search my heart and show me anything that has displeased Your heart in any way. I pray that You would change both my attitude and my conduct to become more like Jesus—the righteous influencer of faith. In Jesus name I ask and pray! Amen!

Application

Brighten up someone's day by helping them with their groceries, giving an encouraging word to the homeless, buying flowers for your next-door neighbor, etc. Giving out of your heart to help someone pleases God more than the devil.

Scripture

Galatians 5:16 (AMP) *But I say, walk habitually in the [Holy] Spirit [seek Him and be responsive to His guidance], and then you will certainly not carry out the desire of the sinful nature [which responds impulsively without regard for God and his precepts].*

After doing one of the actions under Application, or doing something kind for someone else, journal about your experience—what you did, how you felt, how the other person responded, and what you learned, if applicable.

Day 9

What Can We Fast About?

Devotional

What you put into your body and mind affects what comes out. God has asked us to consider fasting, or refraining from something (usually food, but could be your phone, social media, gossip, etc.), and devoting that time to Him through reading His Word, prayer, and worship. Fasting is a disease eliminating, spiritual heart humbling, flesh reducing, faith building, body cleansing, gluttony shrinking action. I fast so I can focus on hearing from God how to overcome sins such as: lust, fear, greed, worry, bad pain, hurt, pride, etc. I can also pray and worship during the fast to draw closer in my relationship with God. Our hearts can become clean when our flesh dies slowly by fasting.

Prayer

Father God, I thank You for helping me understand fasting. I pray that when I fast, You would speak to me about those things I should fast about, when, and how I should fast. I trust You Lord to cleanse my body from any unclean eating that may have affected my system. I trust You, Lord, when it comes to eating healthy and fasting right. In Jesus name I ask and pray! Amen!

Application

Pray about fasting, wait on God to hear how He wants you to fast. Does He want you to fast from food? How long? Does He want you to fast from Facebook or Instagram? For how many days?

Scripture

Matthew 6:16 (AMP) *And whenever you are fasting, do not look gloomy like the hypocrites, for they put on a sad and dismal face [like actors, discoloring their faces with ashes or dirt] so that their fasting may be seen by men. I assure you and most solemnly say to you, they [already] have their reward in full.*

Reflect on the Application section above. If fasting is new for you, consider fasting from just one meal—but be deliberate about spending that time praying and listening to God. Write down what God says to you and stick to it!

_____

_____

_____

_____

_____

_____

_____

_____

_____

_____

_____

_____

_____

_____

_____

_____

Day 10

Taste the Goodness of God

Devotional

Have you ever tasted something so good you wanted more of it? Or have you ever tasted something so bad you wanted none of it? We all have different "taste" buds: style, food, clothes, decorations, hobbies, cars, etc. Our taste can be either sweet or sour. We can taste things that never truly satisfy, like sports, popularity, boyfriends/girlfriends, good grades, etc. OR we can turn our taste to tasting and seeing that the Lord is good. How? When you taste how good God's love is, your taste can change and turn you into a person that's more loving, caring and giving. We can get so filled with the Spirit of God that our senses of joy, love, and peace increase OR we can fill our lives with activities and social media followers so we can temporarily forget about our problems—all of which are silently waiting once we're still, quiet, and alone. Choose today to taste and see that the Lord is good!

Prayer

Father God, I come to You because I want to taste and see that You are good. I want to know what that taste is. God, fill me up with Your Holy Spirit so I never get tired of tasting Your goodness, love, joy, and peace. You can provide all that I need. Turn my heart from liking the taste of this world to loving the taste of You. In Jesus name I ask and pray! Amen!

Application

Take some time in your schedule to spend time with God every day doing what He wants you to do. It can be devotional reading, worshipping, reading the Bible or watching a PureFlix movie with the Lord. Ask Him daily to fill you up with His Holy Spirit.

Scripture

Psalms 34:8 (AMP) O taste and see that the Lord [our God] is good; How blessed [fortunate, prosperous, and favored by God] is the man who takes refuge in Him.

In what ways did you spend time with God this week? Write them down and journal ways He filled you with His Holy Spirit.

_____

_____

_____

_____

_____

_____

_____

_____

_____

_____

_____

_____

_____

_____

_____

_____

_____

Day 11

From Jealousy to Joy

Devotional

Have you ever known friends that seem to get all the things they want? Did it make you feel like you're the only person that never gets those things and left you feeling envious of their dreams coming true? People tell you, "Don't worry, be happy!" You think, *How can I be happy?*

Can I tell you a secret? Jesus. Why? When we turn our hearts to God and ask Him to be THE *one* and *only* Lord of our lives, He can give us that good life of destiny and purpose. Seek His heart first every day, and all the things you need in life will be given. Ask Him to give you JOY and He will. Have you ever asked in Jesus name?

Prayer

Father God, I come to You with my heart full of stuff that I have been dealing with. I see my friends get everything they want and feel like, *What about me? I need things, too.* Lord change my heart and give me a heart that is joyful for them. Let me be happy for them, even though I don't have the same things they do. I pray I will be content in the things You give me—that's all I need. In Jesus name I ask and pray. Amen!

Application

Keep praying every day for God to change your heart. Be happy for people who live the good life. Get excited for yourself when God blesses you!

Scripture

James 3:14-16 (AMP) *But if you have bitter jealousy and selfish ambition in your hearts, do not be arrogant, and [as a result] be in defiance of the truth. This [superficial] wisdom is not that which comes down from above, but is earthly (secular), natural (unspiritual), even demonic. For where jealousy and selfish ambition exist, there is disorder [unrest, rebellion] and every evil thing and morally degrading practice.*

Have you been jealous of any of your friends? Write your prayer of repentance over jealous feelings. Next, list at least ten of the blessings God has given to you!

_____

_____

_____

_____

_____

_____

_____

_____

_____

_____

_____

_____

_____

_____

_____

_____

_____

Day 12

Tame the Temperature of Temper

Devotional

Have you ever felt angry about something but didn't do anything about it? Did the anger direct you toward things that were *not* right? Or did the anger direct you toward things that *were* right? We can be angry toward seeing someone murdered OR we can be angry by murdering someone. There are both healthy and unhealthy anger we can carry. It's okay to have healthy anger, but it's not okay to stay there for a long time. It's what we do with our anger that makes it healthy or unhealthy. We can either make things worse or better for ourselves and for others. It's truly a choice. What choice will you make today to tame that temper?

Prayer

Father God, you know my heart when I see things that make me angry and make me want to respond out of anger. I ask that You take away the tantrums and fits of anger I have been dealing with. Lord God, I give You this anger that hurts me inside. Heal my heart Lord Jesus on the inside and do a mighty work within me. In Jesus name I ask, and I pray! Amen!

Application

Choose today whom you will serve. Will it be God who gives you the ability to forgive people that make you angry OR will it be Satan who feeds you lies so you hold unforgiveness towards people that may make you want to hurt them?

Scripture

Proverbs 15:1 (AMP) *A soft and gentle and thoughtful answer turns away wrath, but harsh and painful and careless words stir up anger.*

List some occasions when you experienced healthy anger, and some occasions when you experienced unhealthy anger. How can you know the difference, and what steps will you take to let go of unhealthy anger in the future?

_____

_____

_____

_____

_____

_____

_____

_____

_____

_____

_____

_____

_____

_____

_____

_____

Day 13

On Whom are you REALLY Focusing?

Devotional

Do you find yourself focusing on something over and over again that you just can't get off your mind? There are a lot of things that we really, Really, REALLY like and want so bad that we just aren't happy with anything else. It might be something physical, like a new iPhone, video game, article of clothing, etc., or it might even be things like making the varsity team, landing the lead in a play, or the attention of that special classmate. It's okay and normal to have dreams and desires for things we want, but it becomes dangerous when we desire it more than the one who created us—GOD. If we are stuck focusing on it over and over and can't let go of it, we've made it an idol. God is righteously jealous for the people He created. He said it himself in the Bible, *"You shall have no other gods before me."* (Exodus 20:3) We can ask God to search our hearts for anything there that He wants to take out.

Prayer

Father God, I come to You with my heart open. Please search it and show me any areas that I may not even see as a blind spot. I want to be free from worshipping it, and ONLY worship You, Lord God. Keep me focused on You. Take out anything in my mind or heart that is keeping me from worshipping You, Lord God. In Jesus name I ask and pray! Amen!

Application

Do you want to please God today? Begin evaluating your heart every time you come to God in prayer. Reflect on your thoughts the last few days Have you spent more time focusing on God's kingdom, or your own wants?

Scripture

Hebrews 12:2 (AMP) *[looking away from all that will distract us and] focusing our eyes on Jesus, who is the Author and Perfecter of faith [the first incentive for our belief and the One who brings our faith to maturity], who for the joy [of accomplishing the goal] set before Him endured the cross,* disregarding the shame, and sat down at the right hand of the throne of God [revealing His deity, His authority, and the completion of His work].

> Ask the Holy Spirit to show you what has been the focus of your heart recently. Write it down, repent, and renounce it. Throw it in the trash and be done with it! Now ask how you can shift that focus to Him instead. Journal your prayer and His response.

_____

_____

_____

_____

_____

_____

_____

_____

_____

_____

_____

_____

_____

_____

_____

Day 14

For the Love of God or Money?

Devotional

Did you ever hear the saying that "Money is the root of all evil?" Actually, the correct version is a Bible verse that says, *"The love of money is the root of all evil."* (I Timothy 6:10, KJV) Loving money more than God has become common today. We want to win the lottery and never work again. Gambling is an open invitation to people's greedy hearts. We can't function, sleep, eat, or be at peace without money. It controls our lives and we put our trust in it. What God wants is for us to trust in Him—the One who gives everything to us we need to sleep, eat, function, and be at peace. I am not saying that you should not have any money, or shouldn't work to earn money, but ask yourself, *Do I value money more than God?*

Prayer

Father God, you are the bread of life, the air we breathe, the God that provides our every need. I pray that my heart would be about loving You more than loving money. I know You will give me what I need instead of me being full of greed. Set me free from the love of money that takes control and help me trust in You with all of my heart because You are in control, Lord God. In Jesus name I ask and pray! Amen!

Application

When we give to the Kingdom of God through things like our tithes, offerings, and sowing into the lives and ministries of others, we reap blessings. Seeking God and giving more to the Kingdom shows our confidence in Him knowing that we won't ever lack.

Scripture

Matthew 6:24 (AMP) *No one can serve two masters; for either he will hate the one and love the other, or he will be devoted to the one and despise the other. You cannot serve God and mammon [money, possessions, fame, status, or whatever is valued more than the Lord].*

Journal about a time when you gave of your money selflessly as a demonstration of your love for God, and the blessings you experienced. If you've never done this before, try it this week, and journal how it made you feel and the resulting blessings you experienced.

_____

_____

_____

_____

_____

_____

_____

_____

_____

_____

_____

_____

_____

_____

_____

_____

_____

_____

Day 15

Let's Be Honest

Devotional

Have you ever been to court, or seen on TV the witness putting a hand on the Bible while the court official asks them, "Do you swear to tell the truth, the whole truth and nothing but the truth?" After they say yes, no one really knows if they are lying or telling the truth because we were not there when the crime happened. God was there when it happened. The only one that knows the truth is God. Proverbs 6:17 *There are six things the Lord hates...a lying tongue.* Some people lie because they are afraid to tell the truth, or they may want to escape from their chaotic situation. The circumstances don't matter—God still hates lies. God loves honest lips and hearts. When we confess the lying to God, he is faithful to forgive us our sins and cleanse us from them. (I John 1:9)

Prayer

Father God, I confess to You that there may have been times where I have lied but never confessed that to You. I confess all my lying and acknowledge that it is sin. Lord God cleanse my heart of any sin I may have carried throughout my life. Let my heart be soft and my lips be honest. In Jesus name I ask and pray! Amen!

Application

Be honest with God and people. You don't have to tell everyone everything about you, but you should be honest.

Scripture

Proverbs 12:22 (AMP) *Lying lips are extremely disgusting to the Lord, But those who deal faithfully are His delight.*

Journal about an instance where you were tempted to lie, but instead told the truth. What was the result? Take a moment to write a prayer of confession to God.

Day 16

Be Unified

Devotional

The world right now has many people living in depression, fear, anger, and hate. These lead to sadness, loneliness, apathy, offense, and even violence. All these things lead to division. Where can we find peace in the middle of chaos? We can pray and ask God to bring unity in people's hearts. When God changes our hearts to be unified to Him, relationships are reconciled and restored. Unity starts within us first and then spreads to others. Have there ever been times when your heart hurt from situations that you didn't know how to escape? You may have wanted to run away from it instead of dealing with it. When God is involved, we can overcome division, so unity rises. Are there any areas in your life where you want things to be unified and ultimately God be glorified?

Prayer

Father God, I come before You thanking You for unity You can provide and that is needed in our world. I ask You to heal my heart from any pain, hurt, and anger I have experienced in the past that is keeping me from continuing toward the direction You have for my life. I pray that my heart is unified toward the people You created and placed in my path, Lord God. In Jesus name I ask and pray! Amen!

Application

Pray for the people that have mistreated you. Have positive and respectful conversations with people about painful emotions you're keeping inside of you. Try to resolve those situations and reconcile with them. Let everything that you say and do be in love.

Scripture

Psalms 133:1 (AMP) *Behold, how good and how pleasant it is for brothers to dwell together in unity!*

Write down one situation and/or person(s) where you need to reconcile and reestablish unity. Perhaps they hurt you, or maybe you hurt them. Write down a brief statement or two outlining how you will approach them and forgive or ask to be forgiven. Ask for God's help restoring the relationship. Follow through today and see how good reconciliation feels.

Day 17

Obedience Reaps Blessings

Devotional

We have many authority figures in our lives, such as parents, teachers, church leaders, employers, etc. that we can choose to obey or not to obey. When we choose not to obey, we experience consequences. When we obey, we experience blessings. It is important to be obedient to our authority figures, but most importantly we need to obey God. He wants our obedience more than sacrificing (giving up) things out of obligation—and obedience brings joy, peace, and blessings. When God asks you to do something, it's how you respond to His voice that is important. Your responses can be yes, no, or a delayed response, which is basically ignoring Him. A yes is obedience. No and delayed are disobedience. Can you imagine if every person on this planet obeyed God's voice? Our world would become more peaceful, loving, caring, and joyful. Acts of obedience please God's heart and bring us joyful blessings. John 14:23 *Jesus replied, "Anyone who loves me will obey my teaching."*

Prayer

Father God, I surrender my heart to You to listen and obey everything You tell me to do. I pray that I would act on what You say. I choose today to obey the word of God and what You say to me. I yield my heart and ask you to lead my steps in the direction You are calling me. In Jesus name I ask and pray! Amen!

Application

Search and look for Bible verses about obedience and blessings. As soon as you hear God's voice, obey it.

Scripture

John 14:23 (AMP) *Jesus answered, "If anyone [really] loves me, he will keep My word (teaching); and My Father will love him, and We will come to him and make Our dwelling place with him.*

Read I Samuel 15 where King Saul gave the best spoils of war to God for sacrifices, instead of obeying God in destroying everything. Write out verse 22. God rejected Saul as king. His sacrifice instead of obedience gave heavy consequences. Do you think that was fair? Why or why not?

_____

_____

_____

_____

_____

_____

_____

_____

_____

_____

_____

_____

_____

_____

_____

_____

_____

Day 18

Freedom in Forgiveness

Devotional

Forgiving people is the hardest thing to do after they have mistreated, hurt, wronged, abused, or violated you! You feel like you're in a prison of torment due to the thoughts and memories of what went wrong. God has a solution for both your past and present problems. Forgive—even if they are people that you hate or that hate you. It's easy to mistreat, be unforgiving, hold a grudge, and stay stuck in that place. And it's hard to forgive and free yourself from the people that have wronged you. It's up to you to decided what you are going to do about it. Forgiving people is a must because it brings freedom to our hearts and minds. Do you want to be free today? What are you waiting for?

Prayer

Heavenly Father, I come before You thanking You for Your forgiveness. You know all about it and can teach me. It's something I have never done, but it's also something that must be done. Lord, search my heart and tell me who I need to forgive that has wronged me. I open my ears to hearing from You so my heart can be set free. I pray that You would set my heart free from all the past and present hurtful memories that have caused me pain. I ask You God to heal, restore, and fill my heart up with Your joy and peace. In Jesus name I ask and pray! Amen!

Application

Forgiving someone doesn't let them off the hook or mean that it's ok for them to continue hurting you. It lets you experience relief and freedom from hurt, bitterness, and anger so you can experience God's peace. Bless the people that hurt you, out loud, and pray for them every day.

Scripture

Matthew 6:14-15 (AMP) *For if you forgive others their trespasses [their reckless and willful sins], your Heavenly Father will also forgive you. But if you do not forgive others [nurturing your hurt and anger with the result that it interferes with your relationship with God], then your Father will not forgive your trespasses.*

> Take a piece of paper and pen, draw a line in the middle of the paper, write down on one side who has hurt you, the other side what they did to you. Tell God that you forgive them for these things and release them for God to deal with their hearts.

Day 19

Fearless

Devotional

Often in childhood we develop silly but real fears over things that we know we can or should overcome. There are all types of fears: insects, rodents, death, speaking in public, etc. Perhaps only you and Jesus know what makes you afraid. We can take baby steps toward being fearless. Being fearful leads to nervousness, anxiety, depression, and all kinds of disorders. Jesus wants us to bring our fear to Him, even if it feels like a giant that we can't knock down. No fear is bigger than Jesus. God's love is perfect for imperfect people. When we receive and are filled with His love in our hearts, there's no room for fear to be there, too. We can be fearless people by focusing on God's perfect love in our hearts.

Prayer

Lord Jesus, I know I have fears over things which I need to face. I open my heart to You, God, to come face-to-face in dealing with my fears. I now confess, repent, and renounce those fears. Jesus, I give them to You and ask that You replace them with Your perfect love. In Jesus name I ask and pray! Amen!

Application

Overcoming fear is a process. Pray every day in Jesus name to replace your fears with trust in Him. I dare you to courageously face one of your fears.

Scripture

1 John 4:18 (AMP) *There is no fear in love [dread does not exist]. But perfect (complete, full-grown) love drives our fear, because fear involves [the expectation of divine] punishment, so the one who is afraid [of God's judgment] is not perfected in love [has not grown into a sufficient understanding of God's love].*

Write out I Timothy 1:7 and memorize it. When facing a fearful situation, recite this verse and persevere with a sound mind!

_____

_____

_____

_____

_____

_____

_____

_____

_____

_____

_____

_____

_____

_____

_____

_____

_____

_____

Day 20

Repair from Compare

Devotional

Have you ever looked at yourself in the mirror and seen things that you don't want to see? A pimple? Blackhead? Wrinkle? Blemish? Tiny hairs? Spots? What makes it worse is when you look at models in magazines and think, *I would love to look like that or have what she has,* and *why can't I look like that?* You start to compare yourself to them and aren't thankful for the image of God created in you. It's dangerous to compare your looks, body, face, personality, hair, etc. with other people. God created only one person that has *your* features, personality, character, and life. Different people are created to do different things. God loves variety in people—we are all different colors, shapes, and sizes. Embrace who God created you to be!

Prayer

Heavenly Father, I come before you thanking you for creating only one of me. If there was ever a time where I was comparing myself to others, I ask that you heal and repair my heart from comparison. In Jesus name I ask and pray! Amen!

Application

Think about how many different types of flowers God has created. What about all the animals? Is there any reason to expect His greatest creation, people, to all look the same?

Scripture

Psalms 139:13-14 (AMP) *For You formed my innermost parts; You knit me [together] in my mother's womb. I will give thanks and praise to You, for I am fearfully and wonderfully made; Wonderful are Your works, And my soul knows it very well.*

Go to any mirror in your home, write down all the things you see that you love about yourself. It can be gorgeous eyes, beautiful smile, etc. Now without looking in the mirror, write down all the things you love about yourself on a piece of paper—the character traits God has given you. Thank God for the beautiful way He has made you. Encourage yourself today!

Day 21

From Self-Glory to God's Glory

Devotional

Has there ever been a time where God has done something great for you and you just thank and praise Him for taking you out of a difficult situation, or protecting you from an accident, providing financial help for something special, or helping you with a difficult conversation? God gets *all* the praise, honor, and glory for helping you through your messy situations. When was the last time you said, "THANK YOU GOD! That was ALL you!" OR did you say, "I am so glad I got myself out of that." We should carefully examine ourselves to know if we are giving God the praise, thanks, and glory OR if we are praising ourselves. When we know God did something, we honor Him. The word glory itself is recognizing His magnificence

Prayer

Lord God, You are the one that created us all for Your glory. I thank You, Lord Jesus, for creating me for purpose and destiny. All glory goes to You for taking me out of messy situations I have been in. Lord God, let everything I say and do be according to Your will. Let it be pleasing and acceptable to Your eyes. In Jesus name I ask and pray! Amen!

Application

Tell people what God has done for you and let them know this, *I give God the glory for that.*

Scripture

Isaiah 42:8 (AMP) *"I am the LORD, that is My Name; My glory I will not give to another, Nor My praise to carved idols."*

Write down one (or more) times when God has helped you in a specific situation. Thank Him for His provision. Now bring glory to His name by sharing your story—your testimony—with someone else.

_____

_____

_____

_____

_____

_____

_____

_____

_____

_____

_____

_____

_____

_____

_____

_____

Day 22

Stay Humble

Devotional

Have you ever received correction from someone and refused to accept it? Did you feel like, *who are they to tell me that?* Did you wish they didn't say anything because you felt it was unnecessary or even embarrassing to you? It can be difficult dealing with correction or instruction from people that want to help you grow and mature. The biggest thing that can get in the way of you receiving correction is pride. Pride is thinking or feeling, *I don't need to hear truth, correction, or receive discipline, because guess what? I GOT THIS! I can do this on my own, and I don't need anybody.*

This mindset can lead to isolation. The solution is to become humble. Humbleness is when you are open to seeking or accepting counsel, mentorship, or discipleship because you know you need someone sharing their Godly wisdom. Your heart opens to receiving correction without being offended. Correction is important, so when we are called to correct someone else, we should always do it out of love. We need to demonstrate love and humbleness whether we give or receive correction. Will you choose the path of humbleness?

Prayer

Father God, I come to You repenting of my pride that gets in the way of my relationship with Jesus and others. I pray for a humble heart, mind, and soul to You, Lord Jesus. Do a mighty work in my heart, Lord Jesus, to free me from all pride. In Jesus name I ask and pray! Amen.

Application

Come to God in prayer and ask Him to humble your heart and take away any pride getting in the way of your relationship with Jesus. You may want to fast and pray for God to humble your heart, especially if you really struggle with pride.

Scripture

Proverbs 13:10 (AMP) *Through pride and presumption come nothing but strife, But [skillful and godly] wisdom is with those who welcome [well-advised] counsel.*

Write about a time within the last week in which someone tried to correct or reprimand your behavior. How did you respond? Were you humble and respectful, or did you roll your eyes in scorn and dismiss what was said? Write your ideal, humble response and remember that next time you are corrected.

_____

_____

_____

_____

_____

_____

_____

_____

_____

_____

_____

_____

Day 23

Keeping Away from Isolation

Devotional

The cause of isolation is loneliness. Are there times where you feel alone, or that no one understands you? Have you felt like you needed to get away from people just to be by yourself? Some people think they need a boyfriend or girlfriend, in their life to make them feel complete. To tell you the heavenly truth, we are never *REALLY* alone, because God is there even when we don't feel or see Him. He is watching and waiting for you to come to Him—to give your heart of loneliness to Him. Isolation keeps you away from people, places, and things. Drawing near to God keeps you away from isolation.

Prayer

Lord Jesus, I bring You my heart of loneliness. There are times where I felt alone and tried to fill that emptiness with something other than You. Lord Jesus, fill that place with Your Holy Spirit, so I can be filled with JOY and LOVE that keeps me far away from isolating myself from people and You. I trust You Lord Jesus for what You will do! In Jesus name I ask and pray! Amen!

Application

Start a journal and write to God about your feelings when it comes to being depressed, lonely, or insecure. Ask Him questions. Wait to sense His loving response and journal that, too. Seek a Christian counselor for additional help if this is an ongoing struggle for you.

Scripture

Romans 8:15 (AMP) *For you have not received a spirit of slavery leading again to fear [of God's judgment], but you have received the Spirit of adoption as sons [the Spirit producing sonship] by which we [joyfully] cry, "ABBA! Father!"*

Write today about the last time you felt lonely and isolated. Write out and memorize John 14:15-16. Remember the Holy Spirit is with you next time you feel alone.

_____

_____

_____

_____

_____

_____

_____

_____

_____

_____

_____

_____

_____

_____

_____

_____

_____

Day 24

Whose Voice are You Hearing?

Devotional

Remember when you were a little and you would listen and obey what Mommy or Daddy said? You knew their voice and trusted it to love, protect, and direct you. Spiritually speaking, human beings were made to hear spiritual voices, too, specifically, the voice of God. We can also hear the voice of the devil. We need to choose which spiritual voice to listen, know, and obey. We can either listen to the voice of truth from God or the voice of lies from the devil. Every decision, choice, or direction we make, or take is a result of listening to the voices in our head. We can respond to our own thoughts (sometimes OK, and other times not due to inexperience or poor logic), the devil (leading us to lie, steal, kill and destroy—often hurting ourselves or others), or God's voice—the voice of truth (leading us to a peaceful, good, joyful, blessed life). The voice you follow leads you to your destiny—cursed or blessed. Whose voice will you follow?

Prayer

Father God, I come before You to thank You for helping me understand whose voice to trust. I pray that You would help me know which voice is whose and help me tune out Satan's and my voices. Lead me to hearing only Your voice so that any decision, choice, or direction I take comes only from You. In the name of Jesus, I ask and pray! Amen!

Application

Practice listening to God's voice by journaling your question or concern to God and His response. Test His response by going to the Bible to verify it's consistent with His word. You may want to share your journaling with two or three trusted Christian advisors to help verify your journaling is consistent with God's voice in scripture.

Scripture

John 10:27 (AMP) *The sheep that are My own hear My voice and listen to Me; I know them, and they follow Me.*

Try the application exercise. Ask God, *How do You really see me?* Wait to hear Him, then journal His response. God's voice will be consistent with what He says in the Bible, and will encourage, edify (build up), and/or exhort (correct) you.

_____

_____

_____

_____

_____

_____

_____

_____

_____

_____

_____

_____

_____

_____

_____

_____

Day 25

Done with Depression

Devotional

The life we live will have dark storms, learning experiences, happy times, challenges, trials, and tribulations. How we can we overcome those dark times when they occur? Do we let them have their way? Do we allow them to run their course? How do we handle them? How do we respond to them? What can we do? We can come to God, sit before His presence, and let Him take over healing the deepest most depressed areas of our souls. Don't allow depression to overtake you—instead allow Jesus to be your peace, healer, and deliverer from depression. When was the last time you approached Jesus about your pain and depression? Will you come to Him today? It's not too late!

Prayer

Lord Jesus, I am thankful I can come to You when I am facing troubled times. I turned to other things to help heal the pain, but I know I can come to You about it instead to take all my depression and pain away. I allow Your presence to heal me and to set my heart free. In Jesus name I ask and pray! Amen!

Application

Take five to ten minutes out of your day, come to God, and start to pray. Spending time with God will bring you more joy, peace, and love in your heart.

Scripture

Psalm 16:11 (AMP) *You will show me the path of life; In your presence is fullness of joy; In your right hand there are pleasures forevermore.*

List ten (10) things you can be thankful for today. It's difficult to be depressed when you start to develop an attitude of gratitude. Consider keeping a separate journal where you list three to five things every day for which you are thankful.

_____

_____

_____

_____

_____

_____

_____

_____

_____

_____

_____

_____

_____

_____

_____

_____

_____

Day 26

Pay Back Evil with Blessing

Devotional

Have you ever been hurt by someone and thought (or said), *I am going to get them back for the wrong they did to me?* When someone hurts us, our immediate reaction is to get even for what they did just so they can see how they made you feel. As a Christ follower, we don't need to repay evil for evil. What we should do is respect, bless, and be at peace with them because it pleases God. God will be the one to pay back the harm they did to you—in His timing (Romans 12:19). We should not hate our enemies but rather love them by blessing them and letting them see the Jesus in us.

Prayer

Lord Jesus, I come before You with past hurts from people who have hurt me. I pray I would not pay back evil for evil, but rather pay back evil with blessings. I forgive and release them from the hurt they did that caused me pain. I ask You to heal my heart completely from the pain and hurt. Help me to love, bless, and encourage them like Jesus would. In Jesus name I ask and pray! Amen!

Application

Pray for your enemies and fast—seeking God's heart to be able to forgive instead of desiring revenge. Love and encourage them even if they dislike you.

Scripture

1 Peter 3:9 (AMP) *and never return evil for evil or insult for insult [avoid scolding, berating, and any kind of abuse], but on the contrary, give a blessing [pray for one another's well-being...*

Write about a time someone hurt you and you wanted revenge. Now write a prayer to God, trusting in His faithfulness to you and releasing that person to God's correction.

Day 27

For Whom Do You Thirst?

Devotional

A lot of things can demand our attention. It can be anything—cars, sports, people, money, social media, video games, etc. Our minds switch on when we see something that captures the attention of our eyes. We crave, hunger, and thirst for it so much that we might even kill to get it. Nothing else will satisfy. When we don't get it, we will go out of our way pursuing it.

There's nothing wrong with having things we want and need, but we must be mindful and careful that doesn't consume us more than God. Our souls crave something to fill the void that only God can fill. It's okay to be thirsty for God. In fact, we can and should crave God more than the materialistic things of the world.

Prayer

Lord Jesus, I come before You with my heart wanting more of You. I have longed for something I thought I needed, and what I was missing was actually Jesus. I pray that You will fill up that place that has been empty. I need the fresh filling of Your Holy Spirit today. In Jesus name I ask and pray! Amen!

Application

Pray for God to increase a hunger for Him inside of you and read the Bible every day to grow spiritually.

Scripture

Matthew 6:33 (AMP) *But first and most importantly seek (aim at, strive after) His kingdom and His righteousness [His way of doing and being right—the attitude and character of God], and all these things will be given to you also.*

Is there something you've been craving or thirsting for? List it, think about how you could use that in God's service. Now write your prayer releasing that desire to God. Be filled with Him instead. Who knows? He may choose to bless you with that object after all!

_____

_____

_____

_____

_____

_____

_____

_____

_____

_____

_____

_____

_____

_____

_____

_____

_____

_____

Day 28

Cast the Criticism Away

Devotional

There's a difference between being critical and giving constructive criticism. When we are critical of others, it brings more hurt than love. When we give constructive criticism, it brings more love than offense. It's an important distinction in how we can help a person. Are we going to help them out of love OR out of envy or hate? Correcting them out of love helps the person grow toward the purpose of life. Criticizing them out of envy or hate offends the person leaving them stuck with hurt, pain, and shame. Words are powerful and carry weight to speak love or hate (Proverbs 18:21). The more we speak in love, the more those around us can receive love.

Prayer

Lord Jesus, I come to You with an open heart to receive correction when I make mistakes or am wrong about things. Heal my heart from any criticism I've heard from people. Lead me, Lord Jesus, to be more loving to people that need correction. Give me a teachable heart to learn and grow. In Jesus name I ask and pray! Amen!

Application

Take the time to hear from the Holy Spirit so you can give an encouraging word to someone that needs to hear it. It can be friends, a co-worker, a family member, or your neighbor. Be bold about it!

Scripture

Proverbs 15:31 (AMP) *The ear that listens to and learns from the life-giving rebuke (reprimand, censure) will remain among the wise.*

Write out Proverbs 18:21. Memorize it. After doing the Application exercise, record how you felt and the other person's response.

_____

_____

_____

_____

_____

_____

_____

_____

_____

_____

_____

_____

_____

_____

_____

_____

_____

_____

_____

_____

Day 29

Becoming Patient

Devotional

There are times we get very impatient about waiting for anything. It can be waiting in line at the grocery store, in traffic, for class to end, for summer break, to graduate, to get married, to have kids. We just can't wait for that to happen! We rush into things when we get impatient and we end up suffering for the bad decisions we make. When we sow patience, we reap peace. When we sow impatience, we reap suffering. It's best to wait because the best will come. Wait on the Lord

Prayer

Lord Jesus, I have acted impatiently, and it caused things to get worse. I choose to be patient—to be at peace for the things You have in store for me. I know You have destiny and purpose waiting for me. I choose to wait on You for Your plans to come to pass. In Jesus name I ask and pray! Amen!

Application

Pray, wait on God, hear His voice, and take action.

Scripture

Psalms 27:14 (AMP) *Wait for and confidently expect the Lord; Be strong and let your heart take courage; Yes, wait for and confidently expect the Lord.*

Write down an occasion when your impatience made a situation worse. Next write one where your patience made a situation better. Now write out Ephesians 4:2.

Day 30

Winning in Wisdom

Devotional

There's a difference between the world's wisdom and God's wisdom. When we don't know what to do about a decision, making a choice, what to say, what to do, how we say it, or when we say it, we can come to God and ask Him for His wisdom. The world around you will gladly tell you their wisdom that may sound and look good but is ill-advised. God's wisdom will lead you to purity, peace, gentleness, open to reason, full of mercy, good fruit, impartial, and sincere. Which wisdom will you choose?

Prayer

Father God, I come before You with my heart seeking to receive Your Godly wisdom rather than the world's wisdom. I need Your wisdom, God, in every area of my life. Without Your wisdom, I am lost. Help me find Your wisdom in everything I say and do. In Jesus name I ask and pray! Amen!

Application

Come to God and ask for His wisdom daily. Apply His wisdom by doing what He wants you to do.

Scripture

James 1:5 (AMP) *If any of you lacks wisdom [to guide him through a decision or circumstance], he is to ask of [our benevolent] God, who gives to everyone generously and without rebuke or blame, and it will be given to him.*

Are you facing a specific challenge right now where you need God's wisdom? Write out your prayer to Him, seeking His wisdom and journal His response.

www.ingramcontent.com/pod-product-compliance
Lightning Source LLC
Chambersburg PA
CBHW061152040426
42445CB00013B/1663